Mirror, Mirror

Mastering Nonverbal Communication for Lasting Impact

Table of Contents

Chapter 1. Introduction

In the dynamic world we live in, communication is key. But here's the twist: it's not all about words! Prepare yourself for a delightful exploration of the art of nonverbal communication in our Special Report: "Mirror, Mirror: Mastering Nonverbal Communication for Lasting Impact." This engaging report dives into the subtle, yet powerful nuances of body language, facial expressions, and gestures. It brings a fresh perspective on how these elements can greatly influence our personal and professional lives. Uncover how mastering this form of communication can boost your confidence, enhance your interpersonal skills, and lead you to success. Come around, let's dive in, and reflect the best version of you!

Chapter 2. The Silent Dialogue: An Introduction to Nonverbal Communication

A conversation is much more than a simple exchange of words. In fact, research supports that the most impactful elements of communication are nonverbal. Up to 93% of our communication is nonverbal, of which 55% is through body language and 38% involving tone of voice and pitch. It's a silent dialogue that happens in every interaction, an interplay of expressions, gestures, posture, that either reinforce or belie our verbal messages.

2.1. The Roots of Nonverbal Communication

For human beings, nonverbal cues are instinctual and primal. Long before the advent of written and oral language, our ancestors relied on nonverbal signals to express fear, hostility, affection, and other basic emotions or desires. These subtle signals were key to survival, providing vital information about the surrounding environment and social interactions. Over thousands of years, this silent form of communication evolved, integrating seamlessly into the complex communication methods we use today.

2.2. Understanding the Basics of Nonverbal Communication

There are various components that fall within the scope of nonverbal communication. These include body language, facial expressions, gestures, eye contact, touch, physical space, emotional expression (voice tone, pitch), and even time. Encoding these signals is often subconscious, but their impact can be consciously recognized and interpreted.

2.3. Body Language and Posture

Our body language conveys a powerful message, often even before we start to speak. The way we stand, sit, and move reflects our mental and emotional state. Relaxed open postures usually indicate a relaxed and open mindset, while hunched shoulders or crossed arms might suggest discomfort or defensiveness.

2.4. Facial Expressions

Facial expressions often serve as a direct projection of what's going on inside our minds. Happiness, sadness, anger, surprise, fear, and disgust are universally identified through facial expressions. Even if we try to conceal our true feelings, subtle micro-expressions can give us away.

2.5. Gestures

Gestures constitute a sizable portion of our daily communication. They range from conventional signals such as a wave hello or a thumbs up in approval, to more subtle cues like rubbing a forehead when stressed or bobbing a foot when anxious.

2.6. Understanding Eye Contact

The eyes are mystically referred to as the 'windows to the soul.' Eye contact fosters a sense of connection and trust. It entails attention, interest, or even attraction. However, prolonged eye contact can sometimes be perceived as aggressive or confrontational.

2.7. The Power of Touch

Affective touch is a fundamental human need. From a firm handshake to a comforting pat on the back, touch conveys an array of messages. In different cultures, the social touch varies both on context and comfort level.

2.8. Use of Physical Space

The physical space we maintain from others during communication, also known as 'proxemics,' conveys unspoken interpersonal relations or even power dynamics. Personal space varies culturally and individually: what is considered comfortable for one might be invasive to another.

2.9. Voice: The Unsung Hero

Vocal cues, much like facial expressions and body language, carry a wealth of information. The tone, pitch, volume, and speed of our speech reveal our emotions, confidence, and sincerity.

2.10. The Role of Time

Time, although a silent participant, is a powerful nonverbal communicator. It involves the pace of speech, the interval between responses, punctuality, and even the time spent on a task or conversation.

2.11. Cultural Influences on Nonverbal Communication

Just as dialects and languages vary across the globe, so too do nonverbal communication cues. Gestures acceptable in one culture can be offensive in another. Understanding these differences is vital when communicating with individuals from diverse cultural backgrounds.

Nonverbal communication, with its intricate web of signals, has the potential to enhance or disrupt our messages. Mastering it enables us to better understand our interlocutors, express our thoughts and emotions accurately, and forge more profound connections. It's a silent dialogue that speaks volumes, the mirror reflecting the unspoken crux of our communications.

Chapter 3. Reading the Unspoken: Deciphering Body Language

In the vast repertoire of human communication, body language is akin to a wordless orchestra. Unfathomably rich and complex, body language offers a window into an individual's emotions, attitudes, and behaviors. So let's decipher this complex method of expression with a clear understanding of its subtitles.

3.1. Basics of Body Language

Body language is a part of nonverbal communication that involves the use of physical behavior to express or convey information. It might pertain to any movement or posture that has the potential to communicate, including eye behavior, facial expressions, touch, and the use of space.

Understanding body language involves deciphering the meanings behind such gestures and using this information to form an impression or conclusion about others. When these observations are accurately interpreted, they provide a depth of understanding that enhances our interaction and communication with others.

3.2. Decoding Facial Expressions

The human face is incredibly articulate, capable of giving numerous signals through a variety of expressions. Micro-expressions, fleeting moments of genuine emotion, can provide significant insight into a person's feelings and attitudes. Similarly, macro-expressions, which are more prolonged, deliver clear messages about one's state of emotion.

Neuroscientists and psychologists have identified seven universal human emotions that reflect in our faces: happiness, sadness, disgust, fear, surprise, anger, and contempt. Recognizing these common expressions is the first step to mastering body language interpretation.

3.3. Interpreting Eye Movements

Eyes are considered the windows to the soul. Their direction, frequency of blinks, pupil dilation, and focus all hold valuable clues about an individual's emotions, intentions, and even thought processes. Prolonged eye contact often suggests interest and engagement, while averted gaze might denote discomfort or evasion.

Blink rates can also indicate stress, cognitive load, or lie detection. Increased blinking tends to denote deception or discomfort, while steady or slow blinking could reflect composure and confidence.

3.4. Postures and Gestures: Silent yet Powerful

Postures carry more expression than we often give them credit for. A person's stance can express confidence, hesitation, openness, defensiveness, and countless other states. An open posture, with arms and legs uncrossed and torso leaning forward, signals accessibility and engagement. On the contrary, a closed stance with folded arms might conceal anxiety or disagreement.

Gestures are potent means of implicit communication. They range from conventionalized signs such as a thumbs-up or a head nod, to spontaneous and personalized gestures that serve to emphasize or elucidate verbal messages. Observing gestures in their particular context can often unveil their underlying meaning.

3.5. Decoding Touch in Communication

Touch, or tactile communication, serves as an intimate form of nonverbal interaction. The act of touching can communicate varying meanings based on the context, the relationship between the people involved, and the manner of touch. A pat on the back can symbolize encouragement, while a firm handshake often represents agreement or congratulations.

Interpretation of touch should consider cultural and personal boundaries as well as the specific situation in which it occurs.

3.6. Proximity and Personal Space

Respect for personal space is an essential aspect of body language. It plays into our subconscious understanding of relationships, privacy, and comfort. People tend to maintain a comfortable distance, known as 'personal space' with others. Invasion of this space can cause discomfort and can be interpreted as aggression or intimacy, depending on the relation between the two individuals.

Space usage also extends beyond personal boundaries to signify power dynamics. The manner in which people position themselves in relation to others within a room can convey a great deal about their perceived social status.

3.7. Body Language across Cultures

Body language is largely universal, but cultural differences do exist. Certain expressions and gestures can have different meanings in different cultures. For example, maintaining direct eye contact is regarded as straightforwardness in Western cultures but can be viewed as disrespectful in some Asian cultures.

Learning and respecting these cultural differences in body language is essential for effective intercultural communication.

3.8. Deciphering Deception

Understanding body language can also help in lie detection. Micro-expressions, inconsistencies between verbal messages, and nonverbal cues, excessive gestures, and stress signals can indicate duplicity. However, it is essential to remember that these are not foolproof signs of lying but can serve as useful guides.

Provided the nuanced complexity of body language, a comprehensive understanding requires continuous observation, time, and practice. However, as one begins to master its intricacies, the increased depth in communication fosters empathy, understanding, and successful interpersonal relationships. Therefore, the journey to deciphering body language is as enlightening as it is enriching.

Chapter 4. The Subtle Art: Understanding Facial Expressions

In the grand ballet of human interaction, few elements are as telling, as impactful, and as immediate as facial expressions. Studies suggest that we can detect certain emotions in others, such as happiness and anger, from just a fragmentary glimpse of their facial expression. This incredible mechanism of empathy and understanding forms an innate, integral part of what makes us human. This chapter will explore the depth and complexity behind knowing, understanding, and properly interpreting these seemingly swift and involuntary revelations of our internal states.

4.1. Anatomy of Facial Expressions

To comprehend the subtleties of facial expressions, it's important to grasp the basic anatomy behind it. Our face consists of over 40 muscles, uniquely layered and interwoven, creating countless expressions by their numerous contractions and relaxations. Some of these muscle groups bear common names like Orbicularis Oculi (surrounding the eyes) or Zygomaticus Major (lifting the corners of the mouth into a smile). Understanding these muscles and their dynamics will provide a solid foundation for your facial expression interpretation skills.

4.2. The Universal Expressions

According to the renowned psychologist Paul Ekman, there are seven universal facial expressions that are recognized around the globe: happiness, sadness, disgust, surprise, anger, contempt, and fear. Despite different cultures and dialects, these facial expressions remain a global constant. Breaking down and understanding each expression will equip you with a toolkit that can navigate any social situation worldwide.

4.3. How To Decipher Real Expression from Fake

Reality and pretense often blur in the realm of facial expressions. A genuine smile reaches the eyes, crinkling the skin to create crow's feet around them. On the other hand, a fake smile, often dubbed a "social smile" is limited to just the movement of mouth muscles. Similarly, genuine emotions often create facial expressions that are symmetrical and are accompanied by corresponding body language.

4.4. Microexpressions: Window to the Unsaid

Microexpressions are incredibly brief, involuntary facial expressions that last only 1/15 to 1/25 of a second. These automatic flashes of emotion may reveal feelings concealed or suppressed. Despite their fleeting nature, these displays carry a wealth of information with them. Mastering the ability to identify these facial twitches can prove immensely beneficial in professional or personal settings.

4.5. Cultural Differences in Facial Expressions

While there are universal expressions, cultural differences can influence how people express or control their emotions. Compelling research shows that individuals from collectivist cultures, such as Japan or China, are more skilled at controlling their emotional displays to preserve harmony in social contexts compared to individuals from more individualistic cultures such as the United States or Western Europe.

4.6. Facial Expressions in the Professional World

Facial expressions play a vital role in the professional arena. They can validate verbal communication, add weight to your words, and forge strong connections. Understanding and utilizing expressive cues and subtle cues can create a trusting atmosphere, facilitate rapport, and even effectively negotiate and resolve conflicts.

4.7. Facial Feedback Hypothesis

Interestingly, not only do our emotions dictate our facial expressions, but our facial expressions can also impact our emotions. This is known as the "Facial Feedback Hypothesis." This fascinating effect provides a unique perspective on personal development, suggesting how manipulation of facial expressions could potentially influence one's emotional state and overall attitude.

4.8. The Dangers of Misinterpretation

Misinterpreting facial expressions can lead to misunderstandings, strained relationships, and missed opportunities. Recognizing the significant consequences of misinterpretation underscores the necessity to hone the skillset of correctly reading facial cues.

4.9. The Future of Facial Expression Study

Technology is bringing new dimensions to the study of facial expressions. Tools driven by artificial intelligence (AI) can now analyze even the subtlest changes in facial expressions, helping individuals, organizations, and even machines understand human emotion better.

Remember, facial expressions are a language in themselves, closely intertwined with verbal communication, body language, and our internal emotional states. Mastering this art is certainly not an overnight task - it requires practice, patience, and a keen eye for detail. However, the rewards at stake, in terms of improved interpersonal relations and overall personal growth, make it truly worth the effort.

Chapter 5. The Power of Silence: Using Pauses Effectively

In the realm of nonverbal communication, one of the most potent tools at our disposal is often the one we least utilize — silence. Choosing not to verbalize can be a powerful choice, communicating more than words at times. When we opt for silence, or when we deploy it by pausing, we are purposefully articulating without articulation. Pauses can be extremely effective in amplifying the meaning of our communication, creating tension, emphasizing points, and showing respect to the listener.

5.1. Understanding the Value of Silence

In our communication-heavy culture, silence is often perceived as awkward or uncomfortable. However, silence is not merely the absence of sound or dialogue. It is a language in itself that speaks volumes. A well-placed pause can enhance your message's impact, showcase thoughtfulness, and exhibit emotional intelligence.

Silence creates room for processing, reflection, and absorption. When we pause, we naturally allow others to absorb and take in our message. This silent space is essential for processing complex ideas or emotions, enabling the listener to understand and engage more genuinely.

Moreover, silence manifests respect — a pivotal element in effective communication. When you pause, you demonstrate that you value your interlocutor's interpretation or reaction, effectively indicating that you are listening and ready to respond appropriately.

5.2. The Art of Pausing

Mastering the art of pausing necessitates a clear understanding of its different uses and when to employ them strategically. The three primary types of pauses—dramatic, reflective, and instructional, each have unique functions.

- **Dramatic Pause:** Used before an essential point, the dramatic pause amplifies anticipation and emphasis. It's like the still moment before a theatrical climax, underscoring the significance of the forthcoming information. The dramatic pause alerts the listener of an imminent significant point while offering you a moment to gather your thoughts.

- **Reflective Pause:** Typically placed after making an impactful statement, the reflective pause grants your audience time to absorb and contemplate what they've just heard, helping with retention and understanding.

- **Instructional Pause:** Used strategically within training or instructional-based dialogue, this pause allows your audience to catch up, mentally gather the steps or notes required, and prepare for the information to follow.

Leveraging these forms of pauses improves your command over the interaction, transforming it into a more impactful exchange of thoughts and emotions.

5.3. Deploying Pauses in Everyday Conversations

Incorporating pauses into your everyday conversations can significantly enhance the strength and clarity of your communication. Silent moments allow the listener to catch up, assimilate the information, and even prepare a thoughtful response.

Applying pauses is not about inserting forced silences. Instead, it involves understanding the rhythm and the flow of the conversation, knowing when to accent your points with a pause and when to let your words cascade. Once mastered, it adds rhythm to your speech, effectively adding another layer of coherence for the audience.

5.4. Employing Silence in Professional Communication

In the professional realm, the power of silence can be harnessed to forge stronger relationships, influence opinions, and command respect. Providing space for others to voice their thoughts fosters a sense of inclusivity and respect. By consciously pausing during meetings, presentations, or negotiations, you not only enhance your communication but also create an environment conducive to open dialogue.

Equally important is the utilization of silence in one-on-one interactions. An empathetic pause after someone has shared personal information or a thoughtful pause before responding to a request indicates your respect and consideration for the other person's thoughts and feelings.

5.5. The Power in the Pause

In the cacophony of words, silence can hold immense power. Silence, specifically in the form of strategic pauses, can help us express more effectively, accentuate our key points, facilitate better understanding and establish a deeper connect with our audience.

The adage, "Silence is golden," rings particularly true in the domain of nonverbal communication. By mastering when to speak and when to pause, you are well on your way towards becoming a more influential and empathetic communicator, able to create lasting impact through your words and your silences.

Remember, while words may open doors, it is often in the spaces between them where true understanding resides. Harness the power of silence, embrace the pauses in your conversations, and watch your communication skills transform.

Chapter 6. Speaking Without Words: Mastering Gesture Communication

Gestures are powerful instruments in nonverbal communication, capable of revealing thoughts and feelings which words often fail to express. From a simple handshake to a high five, each motion can carry encoded messages that can give our communication nuance, depth, and authenticity.

6.1. Understanding Gestures

Let's start by understanding what gestures are. Gestures are defined as bodily actions or movements of the hands, arms, face, head, or body, designed to express a particular idea or meaning. In general, they can be separated into five categories:

1. Emblems, which are culturally specific and can be understood alone (such as a thumbs up).

2. Illustrators that complement verbal communication (e.g., pointing while explaining directions).

3. Affect displays, which show emotion (such as frowning or smiling).

4. Regulators, which control the flow of conversation (e.g., raising a hand to ask a question).

5. Adaptors, which release mental or physical tension (like biting nails or drumming fingers).

While we all use gestures, the type and frequency can be influenced by cultural background, profession, personality, and context.

6.2. The Importance of Mastering Gesture Communication

Mastering the use of gestures is integral in nonverbal communication for several reasons. First, it can maximize the effectiveness of your message. Aligning your gestures with your words can make you appear more persuasive and your messages more memorable.

Second, understanding others' gestures improves your awareness of their feelings and thoughts. This deeper understanding can enhance communication effectiveness in personal, social, and professional environments.

Furthermore, it can help you control your impression on others. A firm handshake can show confidence, while open arms can signal that you're approachable.

6.3. Using Effective Gestures

Knowing the significance, let's delve into using effective gestures. Remember, gestures are perceived as a whole along with your facial expression, posture, and voice tone. Here are some points to consider:

- Keep it natural: Forced, unnatural gestures can make you appear awkward and untrustworthy. Practice until they become second nature and fit seamlessly within your communication style.

- Use them to complement: Make sure your gestures align with your verbal messages. Contradictory gestures can confuse the receiver and weaken your message.

- Be culturally aware: Be sensitive to cultural differences as not all gestures are universally interpreted.

- Use open gestures: Show openness and honesty by keeping your palms up and arms open. Avoid crossed arm or clenched fists as these can appear defensive or aggressive.

- Emphasize speech: Use gestures to emphasize important points in your speech. For example, you might spherical 'air quotes' when you want to underline irony or skepticism.

6.4. Building Awareness of Gestural Communication

Educating oneself about the meaning behind gestures is crucial. Consider the following:

- Observation: Watch how others use gestures. Observing people in various settings such as in work meetings, social gatherings, or even on public transport can help. These observations will widen your understanding of how gestures vary.

- Actively learn: Research, read books or articles, or participate in seminars or workshops focusing on body language and gesture communication.

- Practice: Use what you learned in your daily life. For instance, during a presentation, intentionally implement hand gestures to emphasize crucial points, and evaluate the response.

6.5. Changing and Adapting Gestures

You might wonder, is it possible to change or adopt new gestures? The answer is, yes! You can consciously decide to change or modify your gestures, much like any other skill set. This might require practice until new gestures feel natural to you. It also requires ongoing awareness, monitoring, and self-evaluation.

Begin the process by identifying your gestural habits. Are there any recurring patterns? Do you notice any awkward, distractive or inappropriate gestures? Once you spot the weak areas, create a plan to change them.

In conclusion, mastering gesture communication can significantly enhance your nonverbal communication skill set. It can improve your interactions, increase understanding, and assist in expressing your thoughts and feelings more effectively. The journey might require commitment and practice, but the rewards are vast and empowering. Remember, your body can talk, make sure it speaks your truth.

Chapter 7. Eyes as Windows to the Soul: Interpreting Eye Contact

Eye contact is a powerful form of nonverbal communication. It can convey many things—trust, attention, respect, or even dominance. But first, what really is eye contact?

Eye contact is the act of looking directly into another person's eyes. In human communication, it plays an essential role in displaying attentiveness, signaling intention, and establishing interpersonal connections. However, the interpretation of eye contact varies across different cultures, scenarios, and individuals.

7.1. The Science Behind Eye Contact

Eye contact is, quite simply, a deeply ingrained social habit. Babies are born with a predisposition for staring at faces, and as we grow and evolve, our attention is particularly drawn to people's eyes. The human brain seems hard-wired to detect and draw crucial information from the eyes—a phenomenon known as the Eye Contact Effect.

Neuroscientific research shows that eye contact can activate the social network of the brain, inhibiting the areas responsible for self-awareness and enhancing those responsible for social cognition. It releases oxytocin, often referred to as the "bonding hormone," in the brain, fostering feelings of connection and trust.

7.2. The Power of Eye Contact

One cannot underestimate the power of eye contact as it is a crucial element in affecting people's perception. Maintaining good eye contact can make people perceive you as more reliable, warm, socially attractive, and confident.

It is also an incredibly potent tool to hold someone's attention. When you hold someone's gaze, you are essentially saying, "I am focused on you; you matter"; causing them to reciprocate that attention.

7.3. Reading Through the Eyes

Interpreting eye contact isn't always straightforward. It's key to pay close attention and tread carefully as the meaning might change depending on the context, duration, and the individual involved.

Prolonged eye contact often signals intense emotion or intention. However, staring can be perceived as aggressive. On the other hand, lack of eye contact could suggest shyness, submission, or disinterest.

In conversation, frequent eye contact is generally a good sign, indicating that a person is engaged and interested in what is being communicated. Conversely, if someone is avoiding eye contact, they may be uncomfortable or want to conceal their emotional state.

7.4. Eye Contact and the Professional Sphere

Eye contact is just as important in the professional world as in your personal life. It's taken as a sign of respect and attention during meetings, interviews, and one-on-one interactions.

In negotiations or conflict resolutions, maintaining solid eye contact displays confidence and demonstrates your dedication to resolving the issue at hand. However, remember not to stare unblinkingly at your opponent—it may be interpreted as a sign of aggression.

7.5. Cross-Cultural Variations in Eye Contact

Eye contact etiquettes are not universally standard and can differ enormously across cultures. What is considered polite or respectful in one society may be seen as rude or hostile in another. For instance, Western cultures usually regard direct eye contact as a sign of attentiveness and honesty. On the flip side, certain Asian cultures might perceive it as rudeness and aggression, prioritizing respectful gaze aversion instead.

7.6. Mastering Eye Contact

Improving your eye contact skills can bring significant gains in both your professional and personal life. However, it is critical to strike a balance—neither avoid eye contact nor hold it too intensely.

Practicing mindful conversation is an excellent step towards achieving this balance. Be attentive to how your counterpart is reacting to your eye contact. If they seem comfortable and engaged, you're likely on the right track.

Eye contact, indeed, is far more than just a mere glance. Its potential ability to connect, communicate, and convert is immense if we unlock it consciously. Eyes truly are the windows to the soul, allowing us to reach out and connect on a personal and emotional level—the key is to know how to interpret and use this powerful tool effectively.

Chapter 8. Invisible Signals: Unlocking the Secrets of Proxemics

To the unfamiliar onlooker, space may seem an inadequate model for study. However, on digging deeper, it becomes evident that this often overlooked aspect of daily interaction carries a wealth of information. The notion of personal space, unspoken rules of distance, the dance of interaction - these all pertain to an area of nonverbal communication named Proxemics.

Established by anthropologist Edward T. Hall in the 1960s, the concept of Proxemics has since shed light on the multifaceted ways in which humans use space as a means of communication, often subconsciously. Divided into the four broad categories of intimate, personal, social, and public distances, Proxemics elucidates the tantalizing hidden code in human interactions.

8.1. Unraveling the Four Distances

Hall's theory of Proxemics is divided into four broad categories based on physical distance.

1. Intimate Distance: Ranging from contact to about 18 inches, this is the space reserved for significant others, close family members, and pets. Communication at this level is distinctly physical, endearing, and intimate.

2. Personal Distance: This spans from 18 inches to 4 feet and is commonly given to friends and acquaintances. We may moderately touch or lean towards the person in this space.

3. Social Distance: At 4 to 12 feet, this space is for regular social interactions at work or in communal places, providing room for

several people.

4. Public Distance: Beyond 12 feet, this applies to lectures, large presentations, and formal events. People communicating at this distance generally raise their voices and use grand gestures to be seen and heard.

While these are more-or-less accepted metrics, individual variations are common, largely influenced by cultural norms and personal comfort levels.

8.2. How Proxemics Affects Interaction

Space, guided by Proxemics, acts as the invisible conductor of the symphony of human interaction. It has the ability to dictate the tonality of an exchange and can fundamentally alter the meaning of verbal communication.

For instance, an extended arm while speaking may indicate openness, whereas folding of hands often shows closed behavior. Crossing into the personal space of a stranger without invitation might be taken as an act of aggression, while doing so with a close friend can communicate comfort and intimacy.

8.3. Interdependencies: Culture, Territory and Context

Culture plays an essential role in interpersonal distances. For instance, Latin American or Middle Eastern societies typically favor closer interpersonal distances, reflecting a high-contact culture. On the other hand, in North American and Northern European societies, individuals prefer more personal space, typifying a low-contact culture.

The concept of territory, too, colors the tapestry of Proxemics. Just as animals mark their territories, humans also subtly mark out areas they consider their own: a teenager's bedroom, the CEO's office desk, or even a regularly used spot in a public park.

Similarly, context or situation also characterizes how space is respected or violated. In a packed subway, the concept of personal space often falls to pragmatics, while in an open park, crossing into someone's personal space might seem invasive.

8.4. Decoding the Language of Space

In the world of business, a seasoned practitioner of Proxemics can gain powerful insights about their associates. A client willing to close a deal may lean forward, bridging the gap, while someone distancing themselves may be uninterested.

In the personal realm, becoming attuned to the subtleties of space can shed light on the dynamics of relationships. A friend who consistently keeps too much distance may be uncomfortable or hiding something, while one who consistently invades your personal space may be attempting to assert dominance.

8.5. Embracing Space: Techniques for Harnessing Proxemics

Artists, whether they are painters, dancers or actors, probably know the most about utilizing space intuitively. But even for those of us who are not artists in the classical sense, learning to use space effectively can be an empowering exercise.

Start by becoming aware of your own space, and how you use it. Practice maintaining open body language and observe how this influences your personal interactions.

It's equally crucial to respect the personal boundaries of others and understand their personal space comfort levels by paying attention to their body language.

So, without us even realizing, our everyday dance through different spaces tells a complex story of our desires, fears, power dynamics, and societal upbringing. Once we unlock this subtle yet powerful language, we can truly add another dimension to our communication skills. Embracing Proxemics can lead to more nuanced social interactions that accommodate other people's comfort and respect their boundaries. Therein lies the beauty of this often overlooked but invaluable aspect of nonverbal communication.

Chapter 9. Creating Lasting Impressions: Nonverbal Cues in Professional Settings

In the wide realm of professional communication, while words are crucial, often, it's the nonverbal cues that mark the difference in making that all-important impression. This complex web of nonverbal expression, built upon facial cues, gestures, posture, and more carries invaluable weight in any interaction.

9.1. Understanding Nonverbal Communication

Nonverbal communication doesn't just supplement what we say orally. It can often set the tone, dictate the nature of interactions, and significantly influence people's perceptions about us.

Think about a professional meeting. The words you speak convey your thoughts, but your body language manifests your emotional state, confidence level, and overall attitude. In such situations, gestures or postures become a mirror that reflects your inner self. On a subconscious level, these cues earn you respect, authenticity, trust, or the opposite, depending on how you use them.

In a professional setting, it's not just about 'what' you say, but also 'how' you say it. Herein, dynamic nonverbals are that vehicle of 'how,' driving your intentions in the right direction, and often, accelerating success.

9.2. Facial Expressions: The Window to Your Thoughts

Perhaps the most telling of all nonverbal cues are facial expressions. Have you noticed how you can often discern whether a colleague is interested in a discussion or a manager is pleased with your work just by looking at their faces? That's the power of facial expressions: they serve as silent yet vocal indicators of our thoughts and emotions.

Mastering your facial expressions can significantly influence how your messages are received and perceived. A warm, genuine smile can make you more approachable. Conversely, a stern or blank face can make you seem unapproachable or disinterested. The magic lies in channeling the right expression at the right moment.

But tread with caution! Misaligned facial expressions can backfire. A smile during a serious discussion, for instance, can be seen as insensitivity. The key is to maintain congruence between your words, tone, and the facial expression.

9.3. Gestures: A Silent Dialogue

Gestures - any movement of your body or face - play a crucial role in expressing ideas or emphasizing points in a conversation. They add depth to your verbal communication, making it more effective and impactful.

Similar to facial expressions, gestures must align with your communication to prevent misinterpretation. For example, when delegating tasks, a firm but gentle hand gesture can suggest authority and commitment. On the other hand, aggressive gestures might be perceived as dominance and a lack of respect.

Remember, cultural differences can influence the interpretation of certain gestures. So, in a culturally diverse workplace, understanding what certain gestures mean to different cultures can prevent misunderstandings.

9.4. Posture: An Upright Attitude

Our posture – whether we stand tall or slouch, make ourselves small or take up space – can convey volumes about our confidence, openness, and attitudes.

A straight, upright posture emanates confidence and authority, making it vital for professional settings. Leaning forward while listening to someone demonstrates engagement and interest, while slouched shoulders may show a lack of interest or even discomfort.

Like any other nonverbal cue, inappropriate use of posture can communicate unintended messages. An overly relaxed posture during a formal meeting can be perceived as disrespectful and non-serious.

9.5. Eye Contact: Windows to Your Interest

Eye contact is another potent nonverbal cue. It not only exhibits your attention towards the person speaking but can also build rapport, exhibit sincerity, and exude confidence.

Maintaining appropriate eye contact during a conversation or a presentation can make your audience feel more connected and respected. But be wary of cultural nuances; while in some cultures, direct eye contact is a sign of trust, in others, it might be seen as rude or intimidating.

9.6. Personal Space: A Breathing Bubble

Our comfort with the proximity of others speaks a lot about our personal boundaries, openness to engagement, and cultural influences. Respecting personal space is crucial, especially in the professional world. Invasions of personal space can lead to discomfort, which may harm professional relationships.

Achieving a balance in defining and respecting personal space can be tricky, given the high level of cultural and individual differences.

9.7. Time: A Silent Communicator

People often forget that how we perceive and handle time is a strong nonverbal cue. In professional settings, a respect for timeliness often correlates to respect for others' time and showcases self-discipline.

Showing up late for meetings or missing deadlines might be interpreted as incompetence or disinterest. On the other hand, being punctual can earn you respect and establish a positive image.

9.8. Appearance and Dress Code: The Visual Impact

Last but not least, your personal appearance and dress code make a significant nonverbal statement about your professional attitudes. Dressing cleanly and appropriately for your work environment can imply respect towards the workplace norms, your role, and your colleagues.

Irrespective of whether your office promotes formal attire or leans towards a casual dress code, aligning with the set norms is essential in maintaining a professional image.

Nonverbal cues are the visual, auditory, and spatial expressions that people observe, consciously or subconsciously. Intentionality in managing your nonverbal communication can greatly enhance effectiveness in professional settings, create lasting impressions and lead down a path of success. It's time to take control of your mirror reflections and shine through these silent communicators!

Chapter 10. The Mirror Effect: Reflecting and Modifying Nonverbal Communication

A mirror can be much more than a reflective surface providing a mirror image of physical appearance. It's an effective metaphor for understanding nonverbal communication. Much like a mirror reflects our image, we, too, reflect our emotions, thoughts, and intentions in our body language, facial expressions, and demeanor. The understanding and adaptation of these reflections are what we term as the 'Mirror Effect.'

10.1. Understanding the Mirror Effect

The Mirror Effect in nonverbal communication refers to how our body language, gestures, and expressions reflect our mental state and how others mimic or respond to this. It derives its name from mirror neurons—the brain cells that fire both when we act and when we observe the same action performed by another.

Humans are naturally inclined to mirror the body language, facial expressions, or attitudes of others. The subconscious imitation can extend from mirroring a simple gesture like a nod to thorough, repeated habits. This phenomenon plays a significant role in how we perceive others and how others perceive us.

A person's nonverbal communication often speaks volumes about their mental state. For example, crossed arms may indicate they are closing themselves off, standing tall may display confidence, and frequent eye contact may suggest trustworthiness.

10.2. The Implications of the Mirror Effect

The way we perceive others and the way we are perceived can have a significant impact on our personal and professional lives. In professional scenarios, say a business negotiation, understanding and adapting your nonverbal cues can make or break the deal. In personal relationships, adapting your nonverbal communication can significantly improve connection and understanding.

10.3. Modifying Nonverbal Communication

As we dive into the power courts of the Mirror Effect, it becomes evident that getting a hold over our nonverbal communication can aid us in showcasing our thoughts and intentions, building rapport, and influencing others positively. So how do we tune our nonverbal cues?

Firstly, cultivating self-awareness is vital. Noticing how you sit, how you hold your hands, your vocal intonation, can all influence the effectiveness of your nonverbal communication. Regularly practicing mindfulness can do wonders for that.

Being situationally aware can also be fruitful. Observing other people's body language and expressions can offer insight into their feelings and thoughts. You can then adjust your behavior accordingly.

Here, the concept of mirroring comes into play. Adapting or mirroring the body language of the person you're communicating with can create a sense of likeness and rapport.

10.4. The Art of Mirroring

Mirroring, when used effectively, can be a powerful tool in establishing meaningful connections with others. However, for it to work, it needs to be subtle and natural. Overdoing it can make the other person feel uncomfortable or that they are being mimicked.

For mirroring to happen seamlessly, being empathetic is the key. When you genuinely care about understanding others, the natural tendency to mirror their expressions and gestures happens without effort.

In a professional setting, it might involve mirroring a colleague's way of speaking or body language to enhance rapport. In a personal setting, it might be as simple as returning a genuine smile, or as complex as echoing a loved one's anxiety or joy in your features.

Remember that mirroring is a delicate dance. It needs perfect timing, subtlety, and a positive intention. It's not about outright imitation but creating resonance with the other person.

10.5. The Science Behind the Mirror Effect

Research consistently confirms that body language and behaviors often speak as convincingly—if not more—than words. For the human brain, actions indeed speak louder than words. The discovery of mirror neurons in our brains has caused significant developments in understanding how we perceive nonverbal communication.

These neurons mimic the actions that we observe. So, when we see someone smile, our mirror neurons for smiling fire up too, creating a sensation in our mind that we are also smiling, and we often do! This empathy helps us establish connections and better understand what the other person is going through.

10.6. Workouts for the Mirror

Incorporating certain practices in everyday life can help facilitate better understanding and usage of the Mirror Effect. Here are a few ways:

1. Observing: Sharpen your skills of noticing nonverbal cues by observing others—on a train, café, or even in the living room.

2. Practicing mindfulness: Mindfulness allows you to be present in the moment and aids in understanding and controlling your nonverbal gestures.

3. Role-playing: Assume both sides of a conversation, switching roles frequently. This can provide insight into how different nonverbal behaviors can influence the flow and outcome of a conversation.

4. Watching and learning from influencers: Ted Talks, interviews, and public speaking events can showcase how effectively influencers use body language and nonverbal cues to their advantage.

10.7. In Conclusion

In the end, it's all about being aware of our nonverbal cues and those of others. The more adept we become in mirroring, understanding, and using nonverbal language to our advantage, the better we become in navigating different life situations with ease. As we master the art of reflecting positively, we create a path for success, and more importantly, meaningful human connections.

Chapter 11. Impacting the Future: Harnessing Nonverbal Communication for Success

The rapidly changing world demands constant and effective interaction. Success today is often linked with great communication skills, and nonverbal communication plays a crucial role in this dynamic scenario.

11.1. The Power of Nonverbal Communication

An essential part of our daily interaction consists of nonverbal cues. Gestures, facial expressions, and even how we position our bodies during a conversation can speak volumes. They often express more than words, providing a wealth of information about a person's emotions, thoughts, and feelings.

Often, the impact of nonverbal communication is subconscious. People may not be actively aware of the signals they give or receive, but these cues shape the perception and response of others.

The ability to harness and control nonverbal communication greatly enhances the potential to succeed. It includes understanding its intricacies to intentionally use it as a powerful tool to influence and persuade others, build stronger relationships, and exhibit confidence and authenticity.

11.2. Integrating Nonverbal Signals into Communication

Nonverbal cues have different dimensions, including facial expressions, body movements, gestures, eye contact, touch, space, and tone of voice. Each dimension carries a unique message and influences how our verbal messages are interpreted.

To effectively utilize nonverbal communication, synchronize these signals with your spoken words. For example, if you're explaining a challenging concept, furrowing your eyebrows might show your seriousness about the matter. Similarly, a steady and firm tone of voice backed up by direct eye contact conveys confidence and reliability.

11.3. Decoding Nonverbal Queues

Understanding other people's nonverbal signals is equally important for success. Decoding the messages hidden in their gestures, facial expressions, and tone of voice enables successful interaction, negotiation, and conflict resolution, leading to robust and fulfilling relationships. It requires empathy and alertness to subtle changes in their nonverbal communication.

Patterns are essential here. One-off cues may not always successfully indicate a person's feelings or intentions. However, repeated signals likely provide accurate insights. For instance, continued avoidance of direct eye contact could signify discomfort, while frequent warm smiles often denote friendliness or approval.

11.4. The Effects on Professional Success

In a professional setting, mastering nonverbal cues leads to varying tangible and intangible benefits. Strong, positive body language can help impress during interviews, establish authority in leadership roles, influence decisions during negotiations, and facilitate effective team building.

Simultaneously, being adept at understanding others' signals helps gauge their reactions and feelings. It can aid in identifying unspoken dissatisfaction, enthusiasm, or doubts, enabling us to address these issues timely and accurately.

11.5. The Potential of Nonverbal Communication in Personal Relationships

In intimate and personal relationships, the role of nonverbal communication is profound. Our body language can convey our deepest feelings and emotions more accurately than words can sometimes.

Effective nonverbal communication can build trust and empathy, paving the way for enhanced mutual understanding. It can prevent misunderstandings, resolve conflicts, and lay the foundation for long-lasting and fulfilling relationships.

11.6. The Road to Mastering Nonverbal Communication

Mastering nonverbal communication is a lifelong journey. It involves continual learning, practicing, and self-improvement. It starts with self-awareness, followed by conscious efforts to control and modify one's own nonverbal cues and a keen willingness to understand others. Essential aspects like cultural differences and individual personality traits also warrant considerations.

Regular practice and feedback are key to improvement. Trial and error, observing others, role-playing, and utilizing professional coaching are beneficial strategies. Constructive feedback from colleagues, friends, and mentors helps rectify mistakes and strengthens proficiency.

11.7. Final Thoughts

The role and impact of nonverbal communication in forging successful personal and professional interactions are far-reaching. By learning and harnessing these cues, individuals and organizations can influence their future interactions, ensuring clarity, authenticity, and understanding.

By reflecting the best version of oneself through nonverbal cues, we not only communicate effectively but also make a lasting impression. The silent language of gestures, expressions, and body movements is indeed powerful. When appropriately harnessed, it can unlock a whole new realm of success and fulfillment.

Indeed, mastering nonverbal communication is like coming face to face with an enriching mirror image of oneself and using it as a potent tool to craft desired futures!

www.ingramcontent.com/pod-product-compliance
Lightning Source LLC
Chambersburg PA
CBHW071016260726
48661CB00007B/2992